W9-CCU-216

DAMAGED

Teamwork

Working Together to Win

by
Joanne and James Mattern

Perfection Learning®

Cover design and inside layout: Michelle Glass

About the Authors

Joanne Mattern is the author of many books for children. She especially likes writing nonfiction because it allows her to bring real people, places, and events to life. "I firmly believe that everything in the world is a story waiting to be told."

Along with writing, Joanne enjoys speaking to school and community groups about the topics in her books. She is also a huge baseball fan and enjoys music and needlework.

Joanne's husband, James, enjoys all sports. He is especially interested in sports history, trivia, and statistics.

Joanne and James live in the Hudson Valley of New York State with their young daughter. The family also includes a greyhound and two cats, and "more animals are always welcome!"

Cover Image: Eyewire

Image Credits: AP/Wide World Photos pp. 5, 8, 12, 14, 17, 21, 23, 29, 34, 36, 38, 40, 42, 45, 50, 52

ArtToday (some images copyright www.arttoday.com)

Printed in the United States of America. For information, contact Perfection Learning® Corporation, 1000 North Second Avenue, P.O. Box 500, Logan, Iowa 51546-0500.
Tel: 1-800-831-4190 • Fax: 1-712-644-2392
perfectionlearning.com
Paperback ISBN 0-7891-5514-1
Cover Craft® ISBN 0-7569-0293-2

Table of Contents

Introduction

The world of sports is filled with amazing achievements. Many of these have been accomplished by individuals. But some of the most inspiring have resulted from people working together as a team.

Teamwork is the foundation of many sports. It is inspiring when an individual breaks a record or wins a championship. But it is even more exciting when the cooperation of many different individuals results in a win.

Every player on a team has strengths and weaknesses. The secret to winning is for the team to blend these strengths and weaknesses into a perfect whole. For a team to succeed, its members have to work together. Even if one member is very talented, the team still needs the contributions of its other members to win.

Meet eight of the greatest teams in sports history. Some of these teams were **underdogs**. No one expected them to achieve the goals they'd set for themselves. Others were powerhouses that included some of the most gifted athletes in sports history. But they were all alike in one way. These teams proved that working together is the secret to winning it all.

The New York Jets
1969

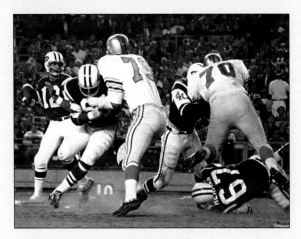

New York Jets (dark uniforms) and Houston Oilers

From 1922 to 1960, there was just one football **league** in the United States. The National Football League (NFL) was the only game in town.

Then, in 1960, the American Football League (AFL) was formed. Most people believed that the AFL would never be as good as the NFL. In fact, many of the AFL's players had been fired from NFL teams. The NFL didn't think they were good enough.

The AFL teams struggled to win games and gain the respect of the fans. But beating the mighty NFL seemed impossible.

Then along came Joe Namath and the New York Jets.

The New York Jets were formed in 1960. They were one of the original AFL teams. At first, the Jets were called the New York Titans. Their first coach was Sammy Baugh. He had been an NFL legend during his days as a quarterback in the 1930s and 1940s.

The Titans got off to a rocky start. Hardly anyone wanted to play for the new team. Even George Izo, the Titans' first-round draft choice, refused to play for the team. Instead, he signed with an NFL team. Many other players did the same thing. The New York Titans' lineup ended up being players the NFL didn't want.

The fans weren't too impressed with the Titans either. The team ended its first two seasons with 7–7 records. But hardly anyone came to see them play.

In 1961, Coach Baugh was replaced with Clyde Turner. This turned out to be a big mistake.

The Titans finished the season with a 5–9 record. It was the worst in the AFL.

Only about 5,000 fans had attended each game. Therefore, the team didn't have enough money to pay its players.

It was only when other AFL clubs chipped in to support the team that the Titans were able to play another season.

At the start of the 1963 season, the New York Titans changed their name to the New York Jets. They also hired a new coach, Weeb Ewbank.

In 1958, Ewbank had led the Baltimore Colts to the NFL championship. Now he was the Jets' best hope for putting together a winning team.

Ewbank didn't waste any time making changes. He let most of the players go and replaced them with younger, newer players.

This new coach also came up with new plays. Many of them were dramatic and tricky. Fans loved the New York Jets. By the end of Ewbanks' first season, attendance at Jets' games had almost tripled from the year before.

Ewbank was always looking for new talent. Soon the Jets had signed some of America's best college football players. Two of the most important were Matt Snell, a fullback from Ohio State, and Joe Namath, an All-American quarterback from Alabama.

Namath's first contract with the Jets paid him $427,000 over three years. This may not sound like much today. But in 1965, it made Namath the highest paid athlete in **professional** sports.

Joe Namath was an exciting player who made things happen. He had a strong arm and terrific aim. He was also able to release the ball quickly during a pass. This helped Namath make split-second decisions and kept him from being *sacked*, or tackled, by the other team. Namath also had a winning personality. His nickname was "Broadway Joe." Namath was very confident. Many people said he was **conceited**. But Namath's bragging inspired his teammates to play better. And his confident attitude was backed up by his ability.

Quarterback Joe Namath drops back to pass in Super Bowl III, January 12, 1969, in Miami, Florida.

Namath won 8 of his first 12 starts in his **rookie** year with the Jets.

By 1967, they had their best record ever at 8–5–1. The only challenge that remained was to win a spot in the Super Bowl and beat the NFL.

The first Super Bowl was played on January 15, 1967. It matched the best team in the AFL against the best team of the NFL. The winner was declared the "world champion."

The NFL's Green Bay Packers had won the first two Super Bowls without much trouble. The AFL teams were badly beaten. One reporter stated that "the AFL is strictly second-class. It will never win a Super Bowl."

The New York Jets dominated the AFL during the 1968 season. Led by Namath's incredible passing, the Jets won the AFL Eastern Division with a record of 11–3. Then they beat the Oakland Raiders in a come-from-behind, 27 to 23 victory to clinch the AFL Championship. The next stop was the Super Bowl!

The Jets faced the Baltimore Colts in the Super Bowl on January 12, 1969. The Colts had lost only one game during the season. Many people believed they were one of the best football teams ever. Everyone believed that the Colts would win and continue the NFL's domination of the Super Bowl—and the game of football itself. Everyone, that is, except Joe Namath.

A few days before the Super Bowl, Namath made an unbelievable statement. He told a group of reporters, "We are going to win Sunday. I guarantee you."

The reporters were shocked at Namath's statement. So were football fans all over the country.

The Baltimore Colts were more than shocked. They were angry at Namath's boast. He had finally gone too far. There was no way the Jets could defeat the mighty Colts.

By the time the game began, the Colts were favored to win by 18 points. Some experts thought they would win by 30 points!

On Super Bowl Sunday, the Jets started slowly. They managed only two **first downs** in the first quarter and were forced to **punt**.

The Colts took control of the ball and jumped into action. They reached the Jets' 19-yard line. But the Colts' quarterback, Earl Morrall, couldn't complete any of his passes. And a 27-yard field-goal attempt by Colts' placekicker Lou Michaels went wide. At the end of the first quarter, there was no score.

The Colts lost another opportunity to score at the beginning of the second quarter. Jets' defensive back Randy Beverly caught an **interception** in the end zone. The Colts were stunned that they had failed to score. For the Jets, the moment gave them even more confidence.

Namath brought the team to life in the second quarter. He kept the Colts guessing by switching between passing the ball and handing it to a teammate. Namath's efforts led to an 80-yard scoring drive. He also completed 3 of 4 passes, including a 12-yard pass to fullback Matt Snell. That pass set up the game's first touchdown. The Jets led 7 to 0. By the end of the game, Namath had completed 17 of 28 passes for 206 yards.

The Jets' **defense** was hard at work too. They intercepted the ball four times and recovered a **fumble** to keep the Colts from scoring. In fact, the Jets kept the Colts from scoring for most of the game.

During the second half, placekicker Jim Turner added three field goals. This increased the Jets' lead to 16 to 0. But the game wasn't over.

Late in the fourth quarter, Randy Beverly intercepted another pass in the Jets' end zone and prevented the Colts from scoring again.

Finally, with just 3:29 left on the clock, fullback Jerry Hill scored the Colts' first touchdown. But that was all they could manage. The Jets won the game—and the Super Bowl—16 to 7. It was one of the biggest upsets in sports history.

There are many reasons why the New York Jets won Super Bowl III. But perhaps the most important reason was that they believed they could do it. Even though the whole world seemed to be against them, the Jets continued on. "You've got to have confidence in yourself," Joe Namath said after the game. "We had confidence in ourselves. We won."

Joe Namath had put his team on the map by leading them to victory in Super Bowl III. But the accomplishment was also a win for the AFL. The league would no longer be considered "second-best" compared to the NFL. Namath and his teammates realized this. After their victory, the Jets were presented with the game ball. But instead of following tradition and giving it to the team's most valuable player, the Jets voted to award the ball to the AFL.

The Miami Dolphins
1972

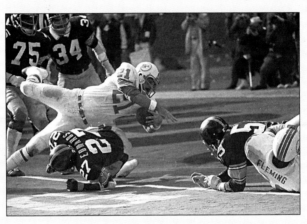

Miami Dolphins (light uniforms) and Pittsburg Steelers

2

Even the best teams lose once in a while. It seems that it would be impossible for any sports team to have an undefeated season. Yet that's exactly what the Miami Dolphins did in 1972. This incredible group of players won every game that season. And they didn't stop there! The Dolphins also won football's highest honor by winning the Super Bowl.

The Miami Dolphins joined the AFL in 1966. For the first few years, they were pretty bad.

Then, in 1970, the team's owner, Joe Robbie, hired Don Shula as his head coach. Shula's hiring was the beginning of a new era for the Dolphins.

Don Shula had a reputation as "football's winningest coach." He had a **knack** for bringing out the best in each of his players and making sure he made the most of their potential.

Before he joined the Dolphins, Shula had led the Baltimore Colts to Super Bowl III. But the Colts lost to the New York Jets. Now Shula was ready to take on a new challenge.

Shula reportedly said, "The only way I know to win is hard work." He drilled his players tirelessly during training camp. And he didn't let up after the season began.

All that hard work paid off. At the end of the 1970 season, the Dolphins were at the top of the Eastern Conference with a 10–4 record. But they lost their first post-season game to the Oakland Raiders, 21 to 14.

Miami won the Eastern Conference again in 1971, with a 10–3–1 record. The team was led by quarterback Bob Griese, placekicker Garo Yepremian, and fullback Larry Csonka. The Dolphins were more than ready to face the Kansas City Chiefs in the American Football Conference (AFC) championship.

After the longest game in football history—82 minutes and 40 seconds—Miami beat Kansas City in overtime by a score of 27 to 24.

Next, Miami destroyed Baltimore, 21 to 0. The team landed a spot in the Super Bowl. But the Dolphins were no match for their opponents, the Dallas Cowboys. The Cowboys won easily. They defeated the Dolphins by a lopsided score of 24 to 3.

Everyone was disappointed by Miami's Super Bowl loss. But no one felt worse than Coach Shula. He told his players to dedicate themselves to getting back to the Super Bowl the next year—and to winning it!

But the Super Bowl wasn't the only goal Shula set for his players. He wanted the Dolphins to win every single game they played during the 1972 season.

Many people thought an unbeaten season was an impossible goal. Shula disagreed.

"I believe you go out every day trying to win," Shula was reported to have said. He didn't want his players to settle for anything less than doing their best.

Shula's team rose to the challenge. They won their first four games, defeating the Kansas City Chiefs, the Houston Oilers, the Minnesota Vikings, and the New York Jets.

But disaster struck in the fifth game against the San Diego Chargers. Starting quarterback Bob Griese was hit by two Charger linemen. He was carried off the field with a dislocated ankle and a broken bone in his leg. It was up to the second-string quarterback, Earl Morrall, to finish the game—and the season.

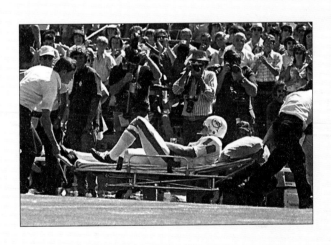

Morrall was 38 years old—ancient by football standards. But he was unstoppable. He completed eight out of ten passes and led the Dolphins to a 24 to 10 victory.

The following week, Morrall and the Dolphins barely beat the Buffalo Bills, 24 to 23.

After that, Morrall settled down. Now the Dolphins were unstoppable! They rolled past all their opponents and easily won their last eight games.

Earl Morrall, called "Old Man" by his teammates, was an invaluable part of the 1972 team. During that season, Morrall led the AFC in passing.

Fullback Larry Csonka and halfback Mercury Morris were an important part of the Dolphins too. They became the first pair of players to rush for 1,000 yards in the same season. Csonka rushed for 1,117 yards, while Morris rushed for 1,000.

Morrall, Csonka, and Morris got the ball downfield. But it was the Miami defense that worked hard to keep the other team from scoring. Miami's defensive team was called the "No Name Defense." They got that nickname because none of the defensive players stood out. They all worked together to stop opposing teams right in their tracks.

By the end of the 1972 season, Miami had achieved its undefeated season. The team went into the **playoffs** with a perfect 14–0 record. But all the players' hard work was almost for nothing.

Facing the Cleveland Browns, Miami was losing 14 to 13, with only eight minutes left to play in the game. Then, led by Morrall's expert passing, the Dolphins came to life and scored a touchdown to win the game, 20 to 14.

Disaster loomed again the following week when the Dolphins faced the Pittsburgh Steelers. Morrall couldn't seem to do anything against the Steelers' defense. The Dolphins were losing 10 to 7.

Finally, Coach Shula pulled Morrall out of the game. His replacement was Bob Griese, whose injured ankle had finally healed. Griese sparked the Dolphins. They went on to score two touchdowns and win the game, 21 to 17.

The Dolphins had made it to the Super Bowl. But they faced a tough opponent in the Washington Redskins. Could Miami continue their unbeaten streak and win the championship?

The Dolphins got off to a quick 7 to 0 lead when Griese threw a 28-yard touchdown pass. Later, safety Jake Scott intercepted a pass from the Redskins' Billy Kilmer and returned the ball 55 yards to prevent the Redskins from scoring. The Dolphins never let up the pressure.

Finally, it was all over. The Miami Dolphins had beaten the Washington Redskins, 14 to 7. They had won their first Super Bowl. They had achieved the impossible, a 17–0 season.

Miami went on to repeat as Super Bowl champions in 1974. And over the years, the team has featured other great players. But no one has ever equaled the 1972 squad and their incredible achievement. At the end of the season, it was reported that Don Shula said, "This is the finest team I've ever seen. Nobody has ever done what this team has done." And it seems likely that no team ever will.

The U.S. Olympic Hockey Team 1980

3

In 1980, America badly needed something to cheer about. Seventy-nine Americans were being held hostage in Iran. The price of everything was up. Many people were unemployed. The U.S. government was angry at the Soviet government for invading the small country of Afghanistan.

The U.S. Olympic Committee was even considering a **boycott** of the 1980 Summer Olympics. They were to be held in Moscow, the Soviet Union's capital city.

In those dark days of February 1980, American athletes gathered in the tiny village of Lake Placid, New York, to compete in the Winter Olympic Games. No one expected the United States to do very well at the Games. The Soviets, on the other hand, were expected to win a lot of medals.

One gold medal the Soviets were sure to win was in hockey. Since 1964, the Soviets had won every Olympic hockey gold medal.

The American team was given little chance of winning any medals. The team was a collection of college and minor-league players coached by Herb Brooks. He was the hockey coach at the University of Minnesota.

But Herb Brooks and his ragtag team had other plans.

When he signed on as the hockey team's coach, Brooks knew he had a lot of work ahead of him. He had to take a group of confident, stubborn young men and teach them how to work together as a team. If his players weren't as naturally talented as the Soviets, Brooks was determined they would work twice as hard to make up for it.

Brooks had his players skate up and down the ice to build up their **stamina** and speed. He made them run as if they were training for a track and field event instead of a hockey game. And he didn't give anyone a break, no matter how tired the player was. Herb Brooks was one tough coach.

Training wasn't the only way Brooks got his team ready for the Olympics. The team played a series of 61 **exhibition**

games. They played all sorts of teams—college, foreign, and National Hockey League (NHL) teams.

The Americans won 42 games. That should have made them pretty confident. But in the last game of the tour, the Americans faced the Soviets. They lost by the embarrassing score of 10 to 3. Everyone expected the same thing to happen during the Olympics.

The Americans finally arrived at Lake Placid. They had been training and playing together for six months. They were friends and teammates. But they still weren't great hockey players. In fact, the team was ranked seventh out of the 12 Olympic teams.

The teams were divided into two divisions. The Americans' first game was against Sweden. Only a few thousand people came to watch.

The Americans trailed through most of the game. But the team came back to end up with a tie. Even though they didn't win, the Americans were pleased with this result. It proved that they could come from behind and not give up.

Next, the U.S. team faced Czechoslovakia. Once again, the Czechs took an early lead. But America's Mike Eruzione scored a goal to tie the game with $4^1/2$ minutes left in the first period.

After that, there was no stopping the U.S. They went on to win—and win big—by a score of 7 to 3.

Suddenly, the Americans—whom everyone had expected to be eliminated by now—were tied with Sweden for first place in their division.

Hockey fans were beginning to notice the American team. Instead of being half filled, the Olympic Ice Arena was packed for their next three games. And the U.S. didn't disappoint their fans. They beat Norway 5 to 1, Romania 7 to 2, and West Germany 4 to 2.

The Americans ended that first round with a record of 4–0–1. That was good enough to move on to the **medal round**.

America's first opponent in the medal round was the dreaded Soviets. The two teams faced off against each other on February 22, 1980. The Soviets had breezed through their division, winning all five games. They would be a mighty foe.

But surprisingly, the U.S. hockey players weren't scared to face the mighty Soviet team. Goalie Jim Craig summed up the team's feelings when he said that they were eager to get a shot at the team. Coach Brooks encouraged this attitude by making jokes about the Soviet players. Doing this meant his team wouldn't take their opponents too seriously.

As usual, the Americans fell behind early in the game, 2 to 1. Then, with just one second left in the first period, American Mark Johnson slipped a shot past the Soviet goalie. The score was tied.

The second period was 20 minutes of tough, physical hockey. The Soviets outshot the Americans, 12 to 2. Amazingly, goalie Craig blocked all but one of those shots. Still, the Soviets were leading 3 to 2 when the teams came out for the third, and last, period.

Over 10,000 fans in the Olympic Ice Arena began to chant, "U.S.A! U.S.A!" Their chants turned to cheers when Mark Johnson scored his second goal of the game to tie the score again.

Then, a little over a minute later, the U.S. team's captain, Mike Eruzione, slammed the puck into the net from 30 feet away.

The crowd—and the team—went wild. Eruzione was mobbed by his joyful teammates. The Americans weren't just winning, they were winning against the "unbeatable" Soviets!

Ten minutes of play still remained. But the heart seemed to have gone out of the Soviet players. They played sloppily. They skated slowly and took wild shots at the American goal. Jim Craig had no trouble blocking those shots and protecting the U.S. team's lead.

The crowd exploded with cheers as the last few seconds ticked off the clock. The spectators waved American flags over their heads. And the entire U.S. team crowded onto the ice, hugging one another and throwing their sticks in the air.

The 1980 U.S. Olympic hockey team upsets the Soviets 4 to 3 in the Winter Olympics, February 22, 1980, in Lake Placid, New York.

Above it all, television announcer Al Michaels screamed, "Do you believe in miracles? Yes!"

The joy of victory spread out of the Olympic Ice Arena and all over the country. People honked their car horns. They cried. They danced in the streets. Total strangers hugged one another and sang the national anthem. Suddenly, the dark cloud that had covered the United States was broken by a beam of light.

The only person not sharing in the celebration was Herb Brooks. He was thrilled at what his players had accomplished. But he remembered the one thing everyone else seemed to have forgotten. The Americans hadn't won any medals yet. They still had one more game to play. It was to be against a strong team from Finland. The winner of that game would go home with the gold medal. The loser would go home with nothing.

Two days after their incredible victory against the Soviet Union, the Americans were back on the ice to face Finland. Once again, they quickly fell behind, 1 to 0.

Each team scored a goal in the second period. But in the third period, the U.S. scored three straight goals to put the game away. The final score was the United States 4, Finland 2. The U.S. hockey team had won the gold medal! Once again, a delighted crowd chanted "U.S.A! U.S.A!"

During the medal ceremony that followed the game, Mike Eruzione, the U.S. team's captain, stood alone at the top of the platform to sing the national anthem. But as soon as the music finished playing, he waved at his teammates to join him on the platform. A group of underdogs had come together as a team to beat the odds and show the world that miracles really do happen.

The Chicago Bulls
1991-1998

Chicago Bulls Michael Jordan, left, and teammate Scottie Pippen

4

Chicago is a city that is big on professional sports. The city features two major league baseball teams, the White Sox and the Cubs; an NFL football team, the Bears; and an NHL hockey team, the Blackhawks. And then there's Chicago's basketball team, the Bulls.

During the 1990s, the Bulls became legendary around the world for their incredible playing style. The team was built around a core of awesome players that included Michael Jordan. It was a **dynasty** that is seldom seen in today's sports world.

But if you had told a Chicago Bulls fan from the 1980s how great the team would be, he or she probably would have laughed at you. Actually, it would have been hard to find a Chicago Bulls fan during the 1980s. In those days, the team was pretty bad.

The Bulls first came to Chicago in 1966 as a National Basketball Association (NBA) **expansion team**. Chicago had had several basketball teams before. But none of them had lasted more than a few years.

The Bulls didn't get off to a very good start either. Only 4,200 fans showed up for their first home game on October 18, 1966.

But the 1966 team was surprisingly good. They even made it to the playoffs—a rare accomplishment for a brand-new team. Even though they lost the championship to the Philadelphia 76ers, everyone agreed that the Bulls could be a great team.

The Bulls did pretty well during the 1970s. But they never managed to win a championship. The team was led by several different coaches during the early 1980s. But no one could lead the team to a winning record.

Everything changed on September 12, 1984. Sportswriters have called that day the most significant day in Chicago sports history.

On that day, the Bulls announced they had signed a gifted

guard from the University of North Carolina. His name was Michael Jordan.

No one had ever seen a player quite like Michael Jordan before. He could do it all—run, pass, shoot, and score. Most of all, he had a fierce desire to win.

One of his teammates called Jordan a "predator" because he was such a tough player. Sportswriters nicknamed him "Air Jordan." He seemed to fly toward the basket and hang in midair when he made his shots.

Along with being a gifted athlete, Jordan also had the ability to motivate his teammates. He became a team leader. And he constantly urged the other players to give the game more than their best effort. At practices, he was the first to arrive and the last to leave. He worked hard. He expected his teammates to do the same.

Most of all, Michael Jordan loved the game.

Fans loved Jordan too. He had a lot of style, a winning smile, and a genuine warmth. Attendance at the Bulls' games almost doubled during Jordan's rookie season.

During his first season, Jordan led the Bulls to their first playoff appearance in four years. Even though the team once again failed to win a championship, Jordan was named NBA Rookie of the Year.

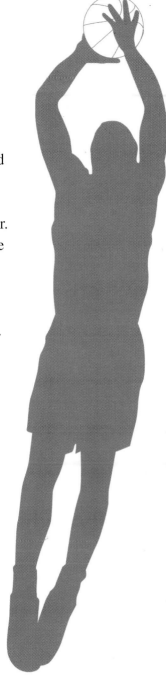

Jordan was a spectacular and gifted player. But he was not the whole team. During the 1987–1988 draft, the Bulls signed two more players who would become a big part of the Bulls' success.

One was Scottie Pippen. The other was Horace Grant. The combination of Jordan, Pippen, and Grant transformed the Bulls into a powerhouse team.

The addition of coach Phil Jackson in 1988 seemed to be the final piece of the puzzle. Jackson was well liked by his players because he treated them with respect. He was always coming up with new ways to challenge them and keep them interested.

Despite the incredible lineup of talent, Chicago had a major obstacle to winning a championship. This obstacle was the Detroit Pistons. The Pistons dominated the NBA in the late 1980s. They also dominated the Bulls, defeating them in the playoffs three straight years in a row.

But by 1991, most of the Pistons' players had passed their **prime**. The Bulls were still young and strong. Led by Jordan's scoring, Pippen's smooth ballhandling, and both players' strong defensive skills, the Bulls finished 11 games ahead of the Pistons to win the title in their division.

Then the Bulls swept the Pistons to reach the championship against the Los Angeles Lakers. It was the first time in Bulls' history that they'd had a shot at the NBA championship.

Now that they had finally made it to the finals, the Bulls weren't about to stop. They beat the Lakers four games to one to win the NBA title.

Jordan became very emotional at winning his first championship after seven years in the NBA. He even broke down and cried after the game.

The Bulls were even stronger in 1992. The team ended the regular season with a 67–15 record, which was the best in the history of the team. They went into the NBA finals against the Portland Trail Blazers.

By the sixth game of the championship series, the Bulls were leading the series three games to two. They needed just one more win to clinch the championship.

But in the fourth quarter, the Bulls were behind by 15 points. Then, led by Jordan and Pippen, the Bulls went on a scoring **rampage**. They scored 14 points, while the Trail Blazers scored only 2. Chicago went on to win the game—and the championship. They became only the second NBA team to win back-to-back titles.

The 1993–1994 season saw an even more dominant Bulls team. They never lost more than two games in a row. They easily made it to the Eastern Conference finals. But many people thought the New York Knicks would win the series. They had a smart coach in Pat Riley and a powerful center and team leader in Patrick Ewing.

However, the Bulls had other ideas. They beat New York. Then they went on to defeat the Phoenix Suns for their third straight championship. It was the first time a team had won three titles in a row in 27 years.

After winning his third championship, Jordan needed a break. He was only 30 years old. But he felt he had achieved all he could as a basketball player.

Jordan had another dream to pursue—and a different challenge to face. He wanted to play major league baseball. So he went off to join the Chicago White Sox, while the Bulls tried to figure out how to go on without their best player.

Scottie Pippen took over the role of team leader after Jordan retired. Pippen played excellently. And the team had added Toni Kukoc, a Croatian who had been the European Player of the Year three times in a row. Yet the Bulls couldn't make it to the championships in 1994.

Meanwhile, Michael Jordan did not have a lot of luck with his baseball career. Although he played in several minor-league games, it was obvious that he didn't really have the talent to compete at that level.

And Jordan's heart was still with basketball. He simply missed playing the game. On March 18, 1995, Jordan thrilled his fans. He announced that he was returning to the Chicago Bulls.

Jordan's return came too late in the season to help the Bulls reach the NBA finals in 1995. But the following season was a different story. Not only was Jordan back, but the Bulls had also acquired Dennis Rodman.

Rodman had a bad reputation off the court because of his outrageous behavior. But he was one of the NBA's all-time best at grabbing rebounds. He had also been part of the champion Detroit Pistons and twice had been named the NBA Defensive Player of the Year.

The combination of Jordan, Pippen, Kukoc, and Rodman transformed the Chicago Bulls into a practically unbeatable team. In 1996, they achieved an unbelievable 72–10 record. It was the best in NBA history.

Chicago Bulls, from left: Dennis Rodman, Scottie Pippen, Coach Phil Jackson, and Michael Jordan

The Bulls dominated the playoffs, losing just one game before the finals. Then they defeated the Seattle Supersonics in six games to win their fourth championship in six years.

"This has been a very, very special year," Jordan told reporters. The players had worked together so well that the only word he could use to describe the team was "amazing."

Toni Kukoc and Dennis Rodman were injured during the 1996–1997 season, but other players were more than ready to step in. The Bulls ended with another incredible record, 69 wins and only 13 losses. Once again, Jordan led the team through the playoffs. The Bulls lost only two games on their road to the finals. Then they faced the Utah Jazz.

The Bulls won the first two games. But they lost the next two on Utah's home court. Game Five was back in Chicago. As the Bulls warmed up before the game, worried murmurs spread through the crowd. Where was Michael Jordan? Why wasn't he practicing with his teammates? Wasn't he going to play?

The answer should have been "No, he would not play." Jordan was sick, either with food poisoning or a bad case of the flu. He hadn't been able to sleep at all the night before. He had a terrible headache, nausea, and a 102-degree temperature.

But even that wasn't enough to stop Jordan from playing basketball. He stumbled onto the court. He looked so weak and sick that the fans were shocked.

Then the buzzer sounded. Game time! Michael Jordan used his illness to motivate himself to another incredible game. By the end of the night, he had scored 38 points. And the Bulls had won the game!

The Bulls went on to win Game Six and the championship, thanks to a last-minute pass from Jordan to his teammate Steve Kerr. Once again, the Bulls were the best!

The Bulls struggled early in the 1997–1998 season. Scottie Pippen couldn't play because of a foot injury that needed surgery.

Despite the fact that he always seemed to be overshadowed by Jordan, Pippen was a vital part of the Bulls. Jordan himself called Pippen "my MVP" when Jordan won the NBA Finals Most Valuable Player (MVP) award after the 1997 championships.

Without Pippen, the Bulls needed Michael Jordan more than ever. He played every game as if it were a do-or-die championship. Jordan pushed his teammates to play that way too.

Dennis Rodman did just that. His rebounding average went from 13 to 17 a game.

Jordan and Rodman led the way. The Bulls began to play harder. And they began to win again. When Pippen returned in January 1998, the Bulls won 10 of their next 12 games. They ended the season with a 62–20 record. They were tied with the Utah Jazz for the best record in the league.

The Bulls cruised past their first two playoff opponents, the New Jersey Nets and the Charlotte Hornets. Their next opponent would be the Indiana Pacers. That's where things got rough.

The Bulls played sloppy **offense** in Game One of the finals. But their defense was terrific. They won the game and went on to win Game Two also.

Then the series moved to the Pacers' home court. A team's chance to win is less away from home, and the Bulls were no exception. The Pacers won the third and fourth games.

When the series moved back to Chicago for Game Five, the Bulls were on fire. They defeated the Pacers, 106 to 87.

The Indiana Pacers played hard in Game Six. Their win tied the series at three games apiece. For the first time, Chicago would have to play a seventh game to win a spot in the championships. Coach Phil Jackson later said this was the toughest series the Bulls had ever faced.

The Pacers had a 20 to 8 lead early in the game. But the Bulls fought back to lead by 2 points at the half.

Back in the locker room, Jordan ripped into his teammates for not playing hard enough. But Jordan himself was getting tired. He made only 9 of 25 shots in the fourth quarter. Still, Jordan refused to be defeated. Led by his incredible willpower, the Bulls won the game. Now it was on to the finals, where they would again play the Utah Jazz.

The Jazz were favored to win the championship. They had easily defeated the Los Angeles Lakers to move on to the finals, so they had a chance to rest while Chicago struggled to defeat the Pacers.

The Bulls did lose the first game. But they came back to win the second game. Then back in Chicago, they destroyed the Jazz, 96 to 54. It was the largest margin of victory in the history of the NBA Finals. The Jazz's 54 points was the lowest score in any NBA game since 1954.

The Bulls and the Jazz split the next two games. Back in Utah for Game Six, the Bulls had a big problem. Scottie Pippen had badly injured his back in Game Three and was in terrible pain. He made a brave attempt to play in Game Six. But he only managed to stay in the game for 7 minutes in the first half and 19 minutes in the second half.

By the fourth quarter, Jordan was in trouble too. He was exhausted. He couldn't make his jump shots. His legs simply had no power anymore.

With 37 seconds left in the game, Utah led 86 to 85. Because they had the ball, it seemed obvious that they would win the game.

But Jordan slipped up behind Utah's Karl Malone and reached around him. He stole the ball! Then, with only 8 seconds left, he faked out a Utah player, drove to the basket, and sank a 20-foot fadeaway jumper to win the game. Once again, the Bulls were champions!

The Chicago Bulls had dominated basketball since 1991. But the dynasty was coming to an end. The players were older, and times were changing.

Phil Jackson left Chicago. He later became the coach of the Los Angeles Lakers. In 2000, he led the Lakers to their first NBA championship in 12 years.

Pippen and Rodman went to play for other teams. And Michael Jordan, who had achieved more in the past seven years than most players achieve in their entire careers, retired for the second and final time.

It was time for another basketball team to rise to the top of the NBA. But no one would ever forget Michael Jordan and the Chicago Bulls.

The U.S. Olympic Softball Team 1996

The U.S. softball team celebrates their 3 to 1 victory over China for the gold medal.

5

Sometimes teams don't have to struggle to be the best. They are already at the top of the heap. But being number one creates its own kind of pressure.

When you're the best, people expect you to win all the time. Many teams can't face this attitude. But some teams perform even better when they know that everyone is counting on them.

One team that did just that was the U.S. Women's Olympic Softball team. They were among the first softball teams to ever play in the Olympics—and the whole world was watching them.

The modern Olympics had been around since 1896. But softball didn't become an Olympic sport until 100 years later.

The road to the Olympics was a long one. In 1965, representatives from the United States, Canada, Japan, and Australia got together to organize the first women's **fast-pitch softball** world championships. For 31 years, teams played around the world. And the United States won almost every championship. By 1996, their record was an impressive 74–9.

From the beginning, the people who organized the women's **tournaments** had one goal in mind. They wanted women's fast-pitch softball to be an Olympic sport.

Finally, the International Olympic Committee agreed. In 1996 in Atlanta, Georgia, softball would be played for the first time as an Olympic sport.

The American Softball Association wanted to continue America's winning tradition. So whoever represented the U.S. at the Olympics had a lot to live up to. The Association spent three years looking for the best American players it could find.

It invited players from the 1995 Pan American Games and the 1995 Olympic Festival. In September 1995 in Oklahoma City, 67 athletes tried out for the team. From that group, 15 women were selected to be the U.S. Olympic Softball team.

For the players, being chosen for the Olympics was a dream come true. Most had been playing softball since they were children. But unlike male athletes, women could not dream of a professional career playing softball. For most of them, softball would be something they would do as a hobby while they worked and raised their families. Playing in the Olympics would be the high point of their softball careers.

Dorothy Richardson was a typical member of the American team. As a child, she could outrun, outkick, and outshoot everyone in the neighborhood—even boys who were several years older than she was.

Dorothy Richardson of the United States, center, celebrates with teammates Laura Berg, right, and Lisa Fernandez.

When Richardson was 13 years old, she became the youngest player in history to join a women's **semipro** softball team. She became the first girl at her junior high to win the school's Outstanding Athlete Award. More awards followed during her high school days. And at age 17, she became the youngest starter on the U.S. Pan American team.

While she played softball, Richardson was also pursuing another dream. She was studying to be a surgeon. She took a leave of absence from medical school to play shortstop for the U.S. Olympic team.

Pitcher Lisa Fernandez was another important member of the U.S. team. In fact, she was considered one of the best softball players in history. What was unusual about Fernandez was that she was a terrific pitcher *and* a terrific hitter. It is very unusual for a player to stand out in both areas.

Fernandez joined her first softball team when she was five years old. Her parents lied and said she was six in order for her to join the team.

When Fernandez pitched her first fast-pitch game, she was only eight years old. And she was terrible! Her team lost the first game she pitched by the embarrassing score of 20 to 0. Fernandez walked almost every batter because she had no control over her pitches. But her parents told her she would just have to work harder to improve. Gradually, Fernandez did just that.

By the time she was 11 years old, Fernandez was pitching for a traveling softball team whose sponsor awarded college scholarships for its best players. She also pitched for her high school team and won many awards.

After college, Fernandez tried out for the 1995 Pan American team. But she didn't perform as well as usual. Still Fernandez wasn't worried. She figured that she would make the top A team because she had played so well in the past.

But the organizers didn't agree. She was placed on the B team. Fernandez was devastated. But once again, she realized that working hard was the best way to solve the problem.

Fernandez went on to pitch a no-hitter and a **perfect game**. She also achieved a stunning .511 batting average. Her performance proved to the American Softball Association that she had what it took to be part of the U.S. Olympic team.

The United States faced seven teams during the first round of the Olympics. They defeated six of those teams—Canada, China, Chinese Taipei, Japan, the Netherlands, and Puerto Rico.

U.S. softball team members from left, Dot Richardson, Lisa Fernandez, and Shelly Stokes

The only team that beat the U.S. in the first round was Australia. Lisa Fernandez pitched eight perfect innings in that game. The U.S. was leading 1 to 0. But in the bottom of the ninth inning, one of the Australian players hit a home run with a runner on base. Australia won the game 2 to 1.

Fernandez was upset at giving up the home run. She thought the loss might cost the U.S. the gold medal. But she could not dwell on losing. There were more games to play.

Fernandez put in a strong performance when she pitched the semifinal game against China. The U.S. won, 1 to 0. Now it was on to the gold-medal game!

The U.S. faced China again in the gold-medal game. A crowd of more than 8,500 people watched the U.S. overpower the Chinese, 3 to 1. Fernandez started the game at third base. But the U.S. pitcher, Michele Granger, was not doing well in the sixth inning. Fernandez was brought in to take her place.

Meanwhile, Dot Richardson hit a two-run homer, and her teammate Kim Maher scored on a single by Sheila Cornell. The U.S. women were Olympic champions!

The U.S. Women's Softball team knew they had done more than win a gold medal. Their hard work and exciting performance opened new doors for female athletes.

Dot Richardson put it best when she told writers, "This one will always be remembered as an opportunity for us to not only represent our country and sport but all women athletes who were not given a chance."

The Tennessee Lady Vols
1997-1998

6

Every year, a fever called "March Madness" strikes sports fans all over the United States. March is when the National Collegiate Athletic Association (NCAA) begins its basketball championships. Over the next three weeks, 64 teams are whittled down to just two. Then those two teams battle for the national championship and the title of the best team in basketball. Two separate championships are held, one for men and one for women.

Usually, it's impossible to pick who will win the championship. Even teams who have done well all season have been eliminated during the run to the championship.

But during the 1997–1998 basketball season, it wasn't hard to guess who would be crowned the best women's basketball team in the nation. The honor had to go to the Tennessee Lady Vols. In fact, they were one of the most incredible basketball teams ever to come onto the court.

By 1998, the Lady Vols already had won the women's title two years in a row. But even those teams weren't as astonishing as the team that tore through the 1997–1998 season. Those Lady Vols were a unique blend of talent, experience, and enthusiasm.

Without a doubt, the star of the team was junior Chamique Holdsclaw, a forward. Sportswriters called her the best player ever in women's college basketball.

Holdsclaw grew up in Queens, New York. She learned to play on the city's playgrounds and outdoor courts, along with dozens of other neighborhood children. Basketball was a popular sport for both boys and girls in Queens. And no one was better than Holdsclaw.

Holdsclaw went on to star at Christ the King High School, which had one of the best basketball programs in the country. With Holdsclaw on the team, the school won four straight state championships.

Holdsclaw received basketball scholarships from colleges around the country. She chose Tennessee for three reasons.

Tennessee's Chamique Holdsclaw

First, she thought the environment would be a nice change from New York City. Second, she liked the fact that Tennessee had a powerful women's basketball program. Finally, she was eager to play under Tennessee's coach, Pat Summitt. Summitt had a reputation as one of the toughest college coaches in the country.

Holdsclaw became the first freshman in Tennessee's history to start every game. She averaged 16 points and 9 rebounds during her first year. She was named to every major All-American team.

During her second year, Holdsclaw did even better, averaging 20 points a game. With Holdsclaw's hard work and terrific play, Tennessee won the NCAA championship in 1996 and 1997.

The Lady Vols added several talented freshmen during the 1997–1998 season. Guard Semeka Randall and forward Tamika Catchings joined Chamique Holdsclaw on the court. The trio soon became known as "the Three Meeks."

Despite the incredible talent of the Three Meeks and the other members of the Lady Vols, Coach Summitt demanded that the women work together. She didn't want a few superstars in the spotlight. She wanted a team. Holdsclaw and the other Lady Vols agreed. They were willing to put the good of the team—and the goal of winning—ahead of their own desire to be stars. This willingness to work together paid off.

The Lady Vols played 39 games during the 1997–1998 season. They won every single one! Their 39–0 record was the best in NCAA history for a men's or women's basketball team.

The Lady Vols didn't just win their games. They won big. Their average margin of victory was 30 points. They beat other Top 5 teams by an average of almost 18 points. In one game, they demolished Georgia by 59 points!

"I haven't seen anyone who can beat them," said Florida coach Carol Ross to reporters after her team lost to the Lady Vols by 39 points. "And I sure hope we don't have to play the team that can."

The Lady Vols usually made winning look easy. But they did run into trouble against the North Carolina Tar Heels during the NCAA tournament. With just 7½ minutes left in the game, the Lady Vols were behind by 12 points.

Then Holdsclaw turned on the power. She made 10 free throws, scored 2 baskets, and stole the ball during a play that put Tennessee in the lead for good. Tennessee won the game, 76 to 70.

Next, the Lady Vols faced Arkansas. Tennessee won easily by a score of 86 to 58. Arkansas was so shaken by the Lady Vols' intense style of play that they turned over the ball 28 times and made less than a third of their shots.

Then it was on to the finals. The Lady Vols had to face Louisiana Tech. Louisiana had an impressive 31–3 record and had won their last 16 games. But none of this mattered once the Lady Vols took the court. The Tennessee team led 42 to 17 by the middle of the first half and won the game by a score of 93 to 75.

Many people thought that Chamique Holdsclaw would leave school to turn pro at the end of the 1997–1998 season. But she didn't. She returned to Tennessee for her senior year because she had promised her grandmother that she would earn her college degree. She also wanted to set a good example for her fans by staying in school.

"I consider myself as a role model," she told reporters. "My responsibility, I feel, is to make [my fans] look at my contributions as a person—someone who is achieving something not just in athletics but in life. Someone who is doing the right thing off and on the court."

Holdsclaw had another reason for finishing college. She was having too much fun with her teammates to quit! "We all get along great," she reportedly said. That sense of teamwork is what made the Tennessee Lady Vols winners.

The U.S. Women's World Cup Soccer Team 1999

Team Captain Carla Overbeck and other members of the U.S. team celebrate after defeating China in the Women's World Cup Final.

7

For years, World Cup soccer has captured millions of fans around the world. But the action usually centers around the men. The biggest fans are in Europe and South America. That all changed in 1999 when a group of women took the United States and the world of soccer by storm.

Until recently, there was no such thing as women's World
Cup soccer. Men had been playing in World Cups since 1930. But
it wasn't until 1991 that eight women's teams met for the first
time in China.

The United States won the championship. But no one paid
much attention. And few people cared when Norway beat the
U.S. in the next World Cup, which was held in 1995.

But women's soccer had been increasing in popularity during
the 1990s. High schools and colleges put more money and
attention into their women's soccer teams.

Slowly, the sport came alive. Players were better. Games were
more interesting. And the fans got excited.

The team that represented the United States in the 1999 World
Cup was a mixture of appealing and interesting personalities.
Perhaps the best-known member of the team was Mia Hamm.

Hamm appeared in advertisements for Nike shoes and Pert
shampoo. She was also named one of the 50 Most Beautiful
People by *People* magazine.

Hamm had commercial success far beyond most athletes,
male or female. She became a role model for thousands of young
soccer fans. These fans mobbed her after her games in order to
get her autograph.

But Hamm wasn't just a celebrity. She was also an incredibly
good soccer player. In 1998, she became the first American and
only the third player in the world to score 100 goals for her
country.

Hamm got her love of soccer from her brother Garrett. Sadly,
Garrett died of a rare blood disorder in 1997 when he was 28
years old. When Hamm played soccer, she played for her brother
as well as for herself and her team.

Hamm made her first appearance on the U.S. team when she

was only 15 years old. She was the youngest player, male or female, to play on a national team. Later, she scored 103 goals at the University of North Carolina, where she led her team to four NCAA titles. She also played on the 1996 U.S. Olympic Women's Soccer team and set up the winning goal in the gold-medal game against China.

Hamm's teammate, Julie Foudy, was another vital member of the U.S. team. She had been playing soccer since she was seven years old.

Foudy had few role models when she was growing up, since most women didn't play soccer in those days. She went on to coach children in soccer camps so that the players of the future would have someone to help them on their journey through the sport.

No soccer team would be complete without a goalkeeper. Brianna Scurry performed that important job for the U.S. team. Scurry was one of the few African American players on the U.S. team. She was also one of the calmest. Even though the responsibility of keeping the other team from scoring created a tremendous amount of pressure, Scurry never panicked or lost her cool.

The U.S. team's coach, Tony DiCicco, first saw Scurry play when she was a junior in college. She made her first international appearance with the U.S. team on March 16, 1994. She had been their starting goalkeeper ever since.

Michelle Akers was the oldest member of the U.S. team. She was 33 years old during the 1999 World Cup. Akers had been playing for the team since its 1991 World Cup days. She also played professionally in Sweden, along with her teammates Julie Foudy and Kristine Lilly.

Unfortunately, by the time the 1999 World Cup was played, Akers was very sick with chronic fatigue syndrome. Despite her illness, she played as hard as she could and never let her team down.

Akers was not the only player who had been with the U.S. team for a long time. Six other players—Mia Hamm, Kristine Lilly, Joy Fawcett, Carla Overbeck, Julie Foudy, and Brandi Chastain—had been on both the 1991 and 1995 World Cup teams. Playing together for so long meant that these women understood one another and worked well together. It also meant that newer players could benefit from the experience of their older teammates. If one player was particularly good at something, her teammates would work hard to master that skill too. All of this made for a stronger team—a winning team.

By the time the 1999 World Cup competition started, the U.S. team was ready for action. And so were the fans. More than 75,000 people showed up to watch the United States beat Denmark by a score of 3 to 0 in the opening game. The U.S. team went on to beat Nigeria, North Korea, and Germany. The team had made it into the semifinals.

The team's opponent in the semifinals was Brazil. Brazil was a dangerous team. Many fans wondered if the U.S. could stop them from scoring. But the U.S. did just that. Defensive players kept Brazil away from the goal. Meanwhile the U.S. scored twice to win the game.

It was time for the finals and time to face China. China would be a hard team to beat. They had defeated the U.S. in two of their last three games. China had played well throughout the World Cup as well. They were ready for any challenges the U.S. team might throw their way.

On July 10, 1999, more than 40 million people watched the game on TV. It was the largest audience for a soccer match in U.S. history. Meanwhile, more than 90,000 fans sat and cheered in the stands of the Rose Bowl in Pasadena, California.

The game turned into a defensive battle. The U.S.'s Michelle Akers threw herself at every ball she could, preventing China from advancing the ball past the middle of the field. In fact, China only got close enough to the American net to make two shots—neither of which went in.

Neither team had scored by the end of regulation time, so the game went into overtime. China made three shots on goal during overtime. The U.S. had a close call when China's Fan Yunji headed the ball toward the left corner of the net.

The ball got past Brianna Scurry, the American team's goalkeeper. But Kristine Lilly leaped forward and headed the ball away just in time.

"Just doing my job," Lilly said calmly after the game.

When the game remained scoreless at the end of two overtime periods, the teams faced off in a **penalty shootout**. China made their first two kicks. So did the U.S. Then Scurry blocked China's third kick. This meant that if the U.S. team could score on their remaining three shots, they would win the game.

Once again, the U.S. made two shots, and China made two shots. The U.S. had one shot left. It was all up to America's Brandi Chastain.

Chastain had been in this situation before. During an exhibition game against China, Chastain had missed a penalty kick. The U.S. had lost the game 2 to 1. That loss had ended the American team's three-year, 50-game unbeaten streak at home.

Chastain blamed herself for letting her team down and losing the game. This time, she was determined things would be different.

Chastain kicked the ball past goalkeeper Gao Hong. The ball curved into the right corner of the net. The U.S. had won the World Cup! Chastain was so happy, she yanked off her jersey and waved it over her head in triumph.

Brandi Chastain, center, celebrates with teammates Sara Whalen, left, and Shannon MacMillan after kicking the game-winning overtime penalty shootout goal against China during the Women's World Cup Final at the Rose Bowl.

In an article for CNNSI.com, Kristine Lilly wrote about the U.S. team. "It was a team that had accomplished its goal. It was a team that stunned the world. It was a team that captured the hearts of millions of Americans. It was a team that did it together."

In the days that followed, all the members of the team became media superstars. Their teamwork and talent had won much more than a World Cup medal. It had changed the way people see women athletes and had given thousands of girls a new goal—to be on a winning team of their own.

The New York Yankees
1999

The New York Yankees celebrate after winning the 1998 World Series.

8 ⚾

How do you follow up a year when you were the best team in baseball? That's easy. You turn around and do it again! At least that's what the New York Yankees did during the 1999 season.

During the 1998 season, the Yankees won an incredible 114 games. Then they swept the World Series, beating the San

Diego Padres in four straight games. They were nicknamed "The Best Team Ever."

But being so good in 1998 put a lot of pressure on the 1999 team. Everyone wondered if that year's team could be as good as they'd been the year before. Because most of the Yankees returned, rather than being traded to other teams, fans were optimistic. And they were right!

The 1999 Yankees won 98 games. While that wasn't as many as the year before, it was enough to get them to the World Series. And once again, the Yankees swept the Series, beating the Atlanta Braves in just four games. It was their third World Series win in four years.

Many people believed that the secret to the Yankees' success was the way every player contributed to the team. Instead of one dominant pitcher or one superstar hitter, every player was incredibly talented.

The team's relief pitcher Mariano Rivera told reporters, "These 25 guys in here are MVPs. It takes 25 guys to do it. That's why we are the Yankees. We play as a group, as a team."

The Yankees faced many tough opponents on the baseball field. But they faced even tougher challenges in their personal lives. The 1999 season got off to a rough start.

Just before spring training started, manager Joe Torre was diagnosed with cancer. He missed the first 36 games of the season while he underwent surgery and treatment.

Many people wondered if Torre could concentrate on the game while he faced a serious illness. They also wondered if his

players could focus on winning
while they were worried about their
coach's health. The answer to both
questions was yes. While Torre was
away from the game, he concentrated on his
health and his family. Once he returned to the
team, he concentrated on baseball.

Torre wasn't the only one who faced a personal
crisis during that season. On September 12, third baseman
Scott Brosius' father died of cancer. Then backup infielder
Luis Sojo's father died on October 22, the night before the first
game of the World Series.

Just five days later, on October 27, outfielder Paul O'Neill
lost his father to a heart attack. That was also the day that the
Yankees won the World Series.

O'Neill could have asked for the day off, but he didn't.
Instead, he played his best. When the game was over and
everyone was celebrating, he fell to his knees in the outfield
and burst into tears.

Of course, there were bright moments during the 1999
season as well. On July 18, David Cone pitched a perfect
game. That is one of the rarest events in sports. Cone's game
was only the sixteenth perfect game in baseball history. And it
was only the third perfect game in Yankee Stadium.

Then there was the Yankees'
amazing run through the playoffs and
the World Series. The team started its
post-season play by sweeping the Texas Rangers. Then they
lost just one game to the Boston Red Sox to win that series
4–1.

The Yankees' opponents in the World Series would be the

Atlanta Braves. The Braves were one of the 1990s' most dominant baseball teams. The 1999 World Series was the Braves' fifth appearance during the 1990s. Many people expected a thrilling, down-to-the-wire championship between these two mighty teams.

But it didn't happen. The Yankees dominated the Braves from the start. The Yankees not only won the Series, they swept the Braves in four games. The exhausting, emotional 1999 season had finally ended in victory.

Looking back at his Yankees after the World Series, pitcher David Cone told writers that "We weren't just a team. We were a family." And like a family, the members of the Yankees worked to achieve their goals—together.

Glossary

boycott	to show disapproval of another country's action by refusing to attend events sponsored by that country
conceited	having a extremely high opinion of oneself
defense	players who try to stop the other team from scoring
dynasty	team that succeeds and is considered the best for a long time
exhibition game	practice game that is played for the public before the regular season begins
expansion team	new team that is added to a league
fast-pitch softball	type of softball in which pitches are delivered underhand in a straight line at high speed
first down	in football, the first play in a set of four plays during which a team tries to move the ball forward at least ten yards
fumble	in football, when a player loses control of the ball
interception	in football, when a defensive (see glossary entry) player catches the ball that was intended for a receiver on the opposing team

knack	special ability to do something
league	group of teams that play against one another
medal round	in the Olympics, the final round of play that decides which teams will win gold, silver, and bronze medals
offense	players who try to score
penalty shootout	in soccer, a series of kicks directly at the goal. Each team chooses five players. The two teams alternate turns. The player of one team kicks from a penalty line in front of the goal. The opposite team's goalie defends the goal against the kick. The team that scores the most penalty shots out of five wins.
perfect game	in baseball and softball, a game in which no one on the opposing team reaches first base
playoffs	series of games played after the end of the regular season to determine a champion
prime	most active, successful stage or period
professional	engaged in by persons receiving money
punt	in football, when the ball is dropped and kicked before it hits the ground. This happens on the fourth down after the offense has failed to make ten yards in the first three downs.

rampage	wild action
rookie	athlete who is in his or her first season with a professional (see glossary entry) team
semipro	team that is paid a smaller amount than a professional team
stamina	staying power
tournament	series of games or events that make up a single unit of competition
underdog	predicted loser

Index